America First
A Budget Blueprint to Make America Great Again

APR 0 4 2017

Office of Management and Budget

U.S. GOVERNMENT PUBLISHING OFFICE, WASHINGTON 2017

For sale by the Superintendent of Documents, U.S. Government Publishing Office
Internet: bookstore.gpo.gov Phone: toll free (866) 512-1800; DC area (202) 512-1800
Fax: (202) 512-2104 Mail: Stop IDCC, Washington, DC 20402-0001

ISBN 978-0-16-093762-0

Table of Contents

	Page
President's Message	1
OMB Director's Message	3
Major Agency Budget Highlights	5
Management	7
Regulation	9
Department of Agriculture	11
Department of Commerce	13
Department of Defense	15
Department of Education	17
Department of Energy	19
Department of Health and Human Services	21
Department of Homeland Security	23
Department of Housing and Urban Development	25
Department of the Interior	27
Department of Justice	29
Department of Labor	31
Department of State, USAID, and Treasury International Programs	33
Department of Transportation	35
Department of the Treasury	37
Department of Veterans Affairs	39
Environmental Protection Agency	41
National Aeronautics and Space Administration	43
Small Business Administration	45
Summary Tables	47
Table 1. Proposed Discretionary Caps for 2018 Budget	49
Table 2. 2018 Discretionary Overview by Major Agency	50
Table 3. Major 2018 Budget Changes from Current Law	52
Table 4. Major 2017 Changes from Security Supplemental Request	53

GENERAL NOTES

1. All years referenced for economic data are calendar years unless otherwise noted. All years referenced for budget data are fiscal years unless otherwise noted.

2. At the time of this writing, only one of the annual appropriations bills for 2017 had been enacted (the Military Construction and Veterans Affairs Appropriations Act), as well as the Further Continuing and Security Assistance Appropriations Act, which provided 2017 discretionary funding for certain Department of Defense accounts; therefore, the programs provided for in the remaining 2017 annual appropriations bills were operating under a continuing resolution (Public Law 114-223, division C, as amended). For these programs, references to 2017 spending in the text and tables reflect the levels provided by the continuing resolution.

3. Details in the tables may not add to the totals due to rounding.

4. Web address: *http://www.budget.gov*

AMERICA FIRST

Beginning a New Chapter of American Greatness

A MESSAGE TO THE CONGRESS OF THE UNITED STATES:

The American people elected me to fight for their priorities in Washington, D.C. and deliver on my promise to protect our Nation. I fully intend to keep that promise.

One of the most important ways the Federal Government sets priorities is through the Budget of the United States.

Accordingly, I submit to the Congress this Budget Blueprint to reprioritize Federal spending so that it advances the safety and security of the American people.

Our aim is to meet the simple, but crucial demand of our citizens—a Government that puts the needs of its own people first. When we do that, we will set free the dreams of every American, and we will begin a new chapter of American greatness.

A budget that puts America first must make the safety of our people its number one priority—because without safety, there can be no prosperity.

That is why I have instructed my Budget Director, Mick Mulvaney, to craft a budget that emphasizes national security and public safety. That work is reflected in this Budget Blueprint. To keep Americans safe, we have made tough choices that have been put off for too long. But we have also made necessary investments that are long overdue.

My Budget Blueprint for 2018:

- provides for one of the largest increases in defense spending without increasing the debt;
- significantly increases the budget for immigration enforcement at the Department of Justice and the Department of Homeland Security;
- includes additional resources for a wall on the southern border with Mexico, immigration judges, expanded detention capacity, U.S. Attorneys, U.S. Immigration and Customs Enforcement, and Border Patrol;
- increases funding to address violent crime and reduces opioid abuse; and
- puts America first by keeping more of America's hard-earned tax dollars here at home.

The core of my first Budget Blueprint is the rebuilding of our Nation's military without adding to our Federal deficit. There is a $54 billion increase in defense spending in 2018 that is offset by targeted reductions elsewhere. This defense funding is vital to rebuilding and preparing our Armed Forces for the future.

We must ensure that our courageous servicemen and women have the tools they need to deter war, and when called upon to fight, do only one thing: Win.

In these dangerous times, this public safety and national security Budget Blueprint is a message to the world—a message of American strength, security, and resolve.

This Budget Blueprint follows through on my promise to focus on keeping Americans safe, keeping terrorists out of our country, and putting violent offenders behind bars.

The defense and public safety spending increases in this Budget Blueprint are offset and paid for by finding greater savings and efficiencies across the Federal Government. Our Budget Blueprint insists on $54 billion in reductions to non-Defense programs. We are going to do more with less, and make the Government lean and accountable to the people.

This includes deep cuts to foreign aid. It is time to prioritize the security and well-being of Americans, and to ask the rest of the world to step up and pay its fair share.

Many other Government agencies and departments will also experience cuts. These cuts are sensible and rational. Every agency and department will be driven to achieve greater efficiency and to eliminate wasteful spending in carrying out their honorable service to the American people.

I look forward to engaging the Congress and enacting this *America First Budget*.

Donald J. Trump

A Message from the Director, Office of Management and Budget

I am proud to introduce the "America First" Budget.

While recognizing this Blueprint is not the full Federal budget, it does provide lawmakers and the public with a view of the priorities of the President and his Administration.

The Federal budget is a complex document. However, working for a President committed to keeping his promises means my job is as simple as translating his words into numbers.

That is why you will find here a familiar focus on rebuilding and restoring our Nation's security. Under the Obama Administration, our shrinking military has been stretched far too thin. The military has been forced to make aging ships, planes, and other vehicles last well beyond their intended life spans. The President will reverse this dangerous trend. From rebuilding our Armed Forces to beefing up our border security and safeguarding our Nation's sovereignty, this Budget makes security priority one.

It does so while meeting another of the President's core commitments: addressing our Nation's priorities without sending future generations an even bigger credit card bill.

This 2018 Budget Blueprint will not add to the deficit. It has been crafted much the same way any American family creates its own budget while paying bills around their kitchen table; it makes hard choices.

The President's commitment to fiscal responsibility is historic. Not since early in President Reagan's first term have more tax dollars been saved and more Government inefficiency and waste been targeted. Every corner of the Federal budget is scrutinized, every program tested, every penny of taxpayer money watched over.

Our $20 trillion national debt is a crisis, not just for the Nation, but for every citizen. Each American's share of this debt is more than $60,000 and growing. It is a challenge of great stakes, but one the American people can solve. American families make tough decisions every day about their own budgets; it is time Washington does the same.

Mick Mulvaney

MAJOR AGENCY BUDGET HIGHLIGHTS

The 2018 Budget is being unveiled sequentially in that this Blueprint provides details only on our discretionary funding proposals. The full Budget that will be released later this spring will include our specific mandatory and tax proposals, as well as a full fiscal path.

For instance, the President has emphasized that one of his top priorities is modernizing the outdated infrastructure that the American public depends upon. To spearhead his infrastructure initiative, the President has tapped a group of infrastructure experts to evaluate investment options along with commonsense regulatory, administrative, organizational, and policy changes to encourage investment and speed project delivery. Through this initiative, the President is committed to making sure that taxpayer dollars are expended for the highest return projects and that all levels of government maximize leverage to get the best deals and exercise vigorous oversight. The Administration will provide more budgetary, tax, and legislative details in the coming months.

In the chapters that follow, Budget highlights are presented for major agencies. Consistent with the President's approach to move the Nation toward fiscal responsibility, the Budget eliminates and reduces hundreds of programs and focuses funding to redefine the proper role of the Federal Government.

The Budget also proposes to eliminate funding for other independent agencies, including: the African Development Foundation; the Appalachian Regional Commission; the Chemical Safety Board; the Corporation for National and Community Service; the Corporation for Public Broadcasting; the Delta Regional Authority; the Denali Commission; the Institute of Museum and Library Services; the Inter-American Foundation; the U.S. Trade and Development Agency; the Legal Services Corporation; the National Endowment for the Arts; the National Endowment for the Humanities; the Neighborhood Reinvestment Corporation; the Northern Border Regional Commission; the Overseas Private Investment Corporation; the United States Institute of Peace; the United States Interagency Council on Homelessness; and the Woodrow Wilson International Center for Scholars.

MANAGEMENT

Making Government Work Again

The Federal Government can—and should—operate more effectively, efficiently, and securely. For decades, leaders on both sides of the aisle have talked about the need to make Government work better. The President is taking bold action now to make Government work again for the American people.

As one of his first acts as President, on January 23, 2017, the President issued a memorandum imposing a Federal "Hiring Freeze" and requiring a long-term plan to reduce the size of the Federal Government's workforce. In addition, on March 13, 2017, the President signed Executive Order 13781 establishing a "Comprehensive Plan for Reorganizing the Executive Branch," which set in motion the important work of reorganizing executive departments and agencies. These two actions are complementary and plans should reflect both Presidential actions. Legislation will be required before major reorganization of the Executive Branch can take place, but the White House is best situated to review and recommend changes to the Congress. In roughly a year, the Congress will receive from the President and the Director of the Office of Management and Budget (OMB) a comprehensive plan for reorganization proposals. The White House will work closely with congressional committees with jurisdiction over Government organization to ensure the needed reforms actually happen.

Simultaneously, the Administration will develop the President's Management Agenda focused on achieving significant improvements in the effectiveness of its core management functions. The President's Management Agenda will set goals in areas that are critical to improving the Federal Government's effectiveness, efficiency, cybersecurity, and accountability. The Administration will take action to ensure that by 2020 we will be able to say the following:

1. **Federal agencies are managing programs and delivering critical services more effectively.** The Administration will take an evidence-based approach to improving programs and services—using real, hard data to identify poorly performing organizations and programs. We will hold program managers accountable for improving performance and delivering high-quality and timely services to the American people and businesses. We will use all tools available and create new ones as needed to ensure the workforce is appropriately prepared.

2. **Federal agencies are devoting a greater percentage of taxpayer dollars to mission achievement rather than costly, unproductive compliance activities.** Past management improvement initiatives resulted in the creation of hundreds of guidance documents aimed at improving Government management by adding more requirements to information technology (IT), human capital, acquisition, financial management, and real property. Furthermore, these Government-wide policies often tie agencies' hands and keep managers from making commonsense decisions.

As a result, costs often increase without corresponding benefits. The Administration will roll back low-value activities and let managers manage, while holding them accountable for finding ways to reduce the cost of agency operations. As part of this effort, OMB will review requirements placed on agencies and identify areas to reduce obsolete, low-value requirements.

3. **Federal agencies are more effective and efficient in supporting program outcomes.** Delivering high-performing program results and services to citizens and businesses depends on effective and efficient mission support services. However, despite years of efforts to improve these critical management processes, managers remain frustrated with hiring methodologies that do not consistently bring in top talent, acquisition approaches that are too cumbersome, and IT that is outdated by the time it is deployed. The Administration will use available data to develop targeted solutions to problems Federal managers face, and begin fixing them directly by sharing and adopting leading practices from the private and public sectors. Among the areas that will be addressed are how agencies buy goods and services, hire talent, use their real property, pay their bills, and utilize technology.

4. **Agencies have been held accountable for improving performance.** All Federal agencies will be responsible for reporting critical performance metrics and showing demonstrable improvement. OMB will also regularly review agency progress in implementing these reforms to ensure there is consistent improvement.

Through this bold agenda, we will improve the effectiveness, efficiency, cybersecurity, and accountability of the Federal Government and make government work again.

REGULATION

Cutting Burdensome Regulations

The American people deserve a regulatory system that works for them, not against them—a system that is both effective and efficient.

Each year, however, Federal agencies issue thousands of new regulations that, taken together, impose substantial burdens on American consumers and businesses big and small. These burdens function much like taxes that unnecessarily inhibit growth and employment. Many regulations, though well intentioned, do not achieve their intended outcomes, are not structured in the most cost-effective manner, and often have adverse, unanticipated consequences. Many more regulations that have been on the books for years—even if they made sense at the time—have gone unexamined and may no longer be effective or necessary.

The President is committed to fixing these problems by eliminating unnecessary and wasteful regulations. To that end, the President has already taken three significant steps:

1. **Regulatory freeze.** On January 20, 2017, the President's Chief of Staff issued a memorandum to all agencies, directing them to pull back any regulations that had been sent to, but not yet published by, the Office of the Federal Register; to not publish any new regulations unless approved by an Administration political appointee; and to delay the effective date of any pending regulations for 60 days to provide the Administration time to review and reconsider those regulations. Federal agencies responded by pulling back, delaying, and not publishing all possible regulations.

2. **Controlling costs and eliminating unnecessary regulations.** On January 30, 2017, the President signed Executive Order 13771, "Reducing Regulation and Controlling Regulatory Costs." This Executive Order represents a fundamental change in the regulatory state. It requires Federal agencies to eliminate at least two existing regulations for each new regulation they issue. It also requires agencies to ensure that for 2017, the total incremental cost of all new regulations be no greater than $0. For 2018 and beyond, the Order establishes and institutionalizes a disciplined process for imposing regulatory cost caps for each Federal agency.

   The significant structural reforms instituted by this Executive Order provide the necessary framework for Federal agencies to carry out the President's bold regulatory reform agenda.

3. **Enforcing the regulatory reform agenda.** As a successful businessman, the President knows that achievement requires accountability. That basic principle is the reason the President signed Executive Order 13777, "Enforcing the Regulatory Reform Agenda," on February 24, 2017. This Order establishes within each agency a Regulatory Reform Officer and a Regulatory Reform Task Force to carry out the President's regulatory reform priorities. These new teams will

work hard to identify regulations that eliminate jobs or inhibit job creation; are outdated, unnecessary, or ineffective; or impose costs that exceed benefits.

They will also be responsible for ensuring that agencies comply with the President's instruction to eliminate two regulations for each new regulation; impose no new incremental costs through regulation; and undertake efforts to repeal, replace, or modify existing regulations.

This Order builds upon a widely recognized and bi-partisan consensus that many existing regulations are likely to be ineffective and no longer necessary, and explicitly builds upon the retrospective review efforts initiated through Executive Order 13563. The difference, however, is accountability, and these teams will be a critical means by which Federal agencies will identify and cut regulations in a smart and efficient manner.

The President recently told Americans, "The era of empty talk is over." When it comes to regulatory reform, it is abundantly clear that the President means business. The President has put into place truly significant new structural mechanisms that will help to ensure that major regulatory reforms are finally achieved on behalf of the hardworking and forgotten men and women of America.

The Office of Information and Regulatory Affairs within OMB is already working hard to support the implementation of these critical new reforms, and it looks forward to making sure that they are fully and successfully implemented over the coming months and years.

DEPARTMENT OF AGRICULTURE

The Department of Agriculture (USDA) provides leadership to promote sustainable agricultural production, protect the long-term availability of food through innovative research, and safeguard the health and productivity of the Nation's forests, grasslands, and private working lands based on sound public policy and efficient management. USDA also works to ensure food safety, provide nutrition assistance, and support rural communities. The Budget request supports core Departmental and mission critical activities while streamlining, reducing, or eliminating duplicative, redundant, or lower priority programs where the Federal role competes with the private sector or other levels of government.

The President's 2018 Budget requests $17.9 billion for USDA, a $4.7 billion or 21 percent decrease from the 2017 annualized continuing resolution (CR) level (excluding funding for P.L. 480 Title II food aid which is reflected in the Department of State and USAID budget).

The President's 2018 Budget:

- Safeguards the Nation's supply of meat, poultry, and egg products by fully funding the Food Safety and Inspection Service, which employs more than 8,000 in-plant and other frontline personnel who protect public health in approximately 6,400 federally inspected slaughter and processing establishments nationwide.

- Provides $6.2 billion to serve all projected participants in the Special Supplemental Nutrition Program for Women, Infants, and Children (WIC). WIC provides grants to States for supplemental foods, health care referrals, and nutrition education for low-income pregnant and postpartum women, infants, and children who are at nutritional risk.

- Fully funds wildland fire preparedness and suppression activities at $2.4 billion, 100 percent of the 10-year average for suppression operations, to ensure the resources necessary to protect life and property.

- Reduces funding for lower priority activities in the National Forest System, such as major new Federal land acquisition; instead, the Budget focuses on maintaining existing forests and grasslands.

- Continues to support farmer-focused research and extension partnerships at land-grant universities and provides about $350 million for USDA's flagship competitive research program. In addition, the Budget focuses in-house research funding within the Agricultural Research Service to the highest priority agriculture and food issues such as increasing farming productivity, sustaining natural resources, including those within rural communities, and addressing food safety and nutrition priorities.

- Reduces funding for USDA's statistical capabilities, while maintaining core Departmental analytical functions, such as the funding necessary to complete the Census of Agriculture.

- Eliminates the duplicative Water and Wastewater loan and grant program, a savings of $498 million from the 2017 annualized CR level. Rural communities can be served by private sector financing or other Federal investments in rural water infrastructure, such as the Environmental Protection Agency's State Revolving Funds.

- Reduces staffing in USDA's Service Center Agencies to streamline county office operations, reflect reduced Rural Development workload, and encourage private sector conservation planning.

- Reduces duplicative and underperforming programs by eliminating discretionary activities of the Rural Business and Cooperative Service, a savings of $95 million from the 2017 annualized CR level.

- Eliminates the McGovern-Dole International Food for Education program, which lacks evidence that it is being effectively implemented to reduce food insecurity.

DEPARTMENT OF COMMERCE

The Department of Commerce promotes job creation and economic growth by ensuring fair and secure trade, providing the data necessary to support commerce, and fostering innovation by setting standards and conducting foundational research and development. The Budget prioritizes and protects investments in core Government functions such as preparing for the 2020 Decennial Census, providing the observational infrastructure and staff necessary to produce timely and accurate weather forecasts, supporting the Government's role in managing marine resources and ocean and coastal navigation, and enforcing laws that promote fair and secure trade. The Budget also reduces or eliminates grant programs that have limited impact and reflect an expansion beyond core missions of the bureaus.

The President's 2018 Budget requests $7.8 billion for the Department of Commerce, a $1.5 billion or 16 percent decrease from the 2017 annualized CR level.

The President's 2018 Budget:

- Strengthens the International Trade Administration's trade enforcement and compliance functions, including the anti-dumping and countervailing duty investigations, while rescaling the agency's export promotion and trade analysis activities.

- Provides $1.5 billion, an increase of more than $100 million, for the U.S. Census Bureau to continue preparations for the 2020 Decennial Census. This additional funding prioritizes fundamental investments in information technology and field infrastructure, which would allow the bureau to more effectively administer the 2020 Decennial Census.

- Consolidates the mission, policy support, and administrative functions of the Economics and Statistics Administration within the Bureau of Economic Analysis, the U.S. Census Bureau, and the Department of Commerce's Office of the Secretary.

- Eliminates the Economic Development Administration, which provides small grants with limited measurable impacts and duplicates other Federal programs, such as Rural Utilities Service grants at the U.S. Department of Agriculture and formula grants to States from the Department of Transportation. By terminating this agency, the Budget saves $221 million from the 2017 annualized CR level.

- Eliminates the Minority Business Development Agency, which is duplicative of other Federal, State, local, and private sector efforts that promote minority business entrepreneurship including Small Business Administration District Offices and Small Business Development Centers.

- Saves $124 million by discontinuing Federal funding for the Manufacturing Extension Partnership (MEP) program, which subsidizes up to half the cost of State centers, which provide consulting services to small- and medium-size manufacturers. By eliminating Federal funding, MEP centers would transition solely to non-Federal revenue sources, as was originally intended when the program was established.

- Zeroes out over $250 million in targeted National Oceanic and Atmospheric Administration (NOAA) grants and programs supporting coastal and marine management, research, and education including Sea Grant, which primarily benefit industry and State and local stakeholders. These programs are a lower priority than core functions maintained in the Budget such as surveys, charting, and fisheries management.

- Maintains the development of NOAA's current generation of polar orbiting and geostationary weather satellites, allowing the Joint Polar Satellite System and Geostationary Operational Environmental Satellite programs to remain on schedule in order to provide forecasters with critical weather data to help protect life and property.

- Achieves annual savings from NOAA's Polar Follow On satellite program from the current program of record by better reflecting the actual risk of a gap in polar satellite coverage, and provides additional opportunities to improve robustness of the low earth orbit satellite architecture by expanding the utilization of commercially provided data to improve weather models.

- Maintains National Weather Service forecasting capabilities by investing more than $1 billion while continuing to promote efficient and effective operations.

- Continues to support the National Telecommunications and Information Administration (NTIA) in representing the United States interest at multi-stakeholder forums on internet governance and digital commerce. The Budget supports the commercial sector's development of next generation wireless services by funding NTIA's mission of evaluating and ensuring the efficient use of spectrum by Government users.

DEPARTMENT OF DEFENSE

The Department of Defense (DOD) provides the military forces needed to deter war and to protect the security of the United States. The budget for DOD ends the depletion of our military and pursues peace through strength, honoring the Federal Government's first responsibility: to protect the Nation. It fully repeals the defense sequestration, while providing the needed resources for accelerating the defeat of the Islamic State of Iraq and Syria (ISIS) and for beginning to rebuild the U.S. Armed Forces.

The President's 2018 Budget requests $639 billion for DOD, a $52 billion increase from the 2017 annualized CR level. The total includes $574 billion for the base budget, a 10 percent increase from the 2017 annualized CR level, and $65 billion for Overseas Contingency Operations.

The President's 2018 Budget:

- Repeals the defense sequestration by restoring $52 billion to DOD, as well as $2 billion to other national defense programs outside DOD, for a $54 billion total increase for national defense discretionary budget authority above the sequestration level budget cap. When the Budget Control Act (BCA) of 2011 was enacted, the defense sequestration was not meant to occur, yet it has never been fully repealed. This has resulted in nearly $200 billion of national defense cuts since 2013 and over $200 billion of further projected cuts through 2021, relative to the original BCA caps alone. Reversing this indiscriminate neglect of the last administration is not only a fulfillment of the President's promise, but it is also a requirement if this Nation's security is to be maintained. The military's depletion under President Obama is our foremost challenge. The President's 2018 Budget ends the arbitrary depletion of our strength and security, and begins to rebuild the U.S. Armed Forces.

- Increases DOD's budget authority by $52 billion above the current 2017 level of $587 billion. This increase alone exceeds the entire defense budget of most countries, and would be one of the largest one-year DOD increases in American history. It is exceeded only by the peak increases of the Reagan Administration and a few of the largest defense increases during the World Wars and the conflicts in Korea, Vietnam, Iraq, and Afghanistan (in constant dollars, based on GDP chained price index). Unlike spending increases for war, which mostly consume resources in combat, the increases in the President's Budget primarily invest in a stronger military.

- Provides the resources needed to accelerate the defeat of ISIS. The Budget ensures that DOD has the tools to stop ISIS from posing a threat to the United States by funding the Department's critical efforts to strike ISIS targets, support our partners fighting on the ground, disrupt ISIS' external operations, and cut off its financing.

- Addresses urgent warfighting readiness needs. Fifteen years of conflict, accompanied in recent years by budget cuts, have stressed the Armed Forces. The President's Budget would ensure we remain the best led, best equipped, and most ready force in the world.

- Begins to rebuild the U.S. Armed Forces by addressing pressing shortfalls, such as insufficient stocks of critical munitions, personnel gaps, deferred maintenance and modernization, cyber vulnerabilities, and degraded facilities. The military must reset war losses, address recapitalization and maintenance requirements, and recover from years of deferred investment forced by budget cuts. The President's Budget would ensure the Armed Forces have the training, equipment, and infrastructure they need.

- Lays the groundwork for a larger, more capable, and more lethal joint force, driven by a new National Defense Strategy that recognizes the need for American superiority not only on land, at sea, in the air, and in space, but also in cyberspace. As the world has become more dangerous—through the rise of advanced potential adversaries, the spread of destructive technology, and the expansion of terrorism—our military has gotten smaller and its technological edge has eroded. The President's Budget begins to put an end to this trend, reversing force reductions and restoring critical investments.

- Initiates an ambitious reform agenda to build a military that is as effective and efficient as possible, and underscores the President's commitment to reduce the costs of military programs wherever feasible.

- Strengthens the U.S. Army by rebuilding readiness, reversing end strength reductions, and preparing for future challenges. This Budget is an initial step toward restoring an Army that has been stressed by high operational demand and constrained funding levels in recent years.

- Rebuilds the U.S. Navy to better address current and future threats by increasing the total number of ships. This Budget reflects a down payment on the President's commitment to expanding the fleet.

- Ensures a ready and fully equipped Marine Corps. The Budget lays the foundation for a force that meets the challenges of the 21st Century.

- Accelerates Air Force efforts to improve tactical air fleet readiness, ensure technical superiority, and repair aging infrastructure. Key investments in maintenance capacity, training systems, and additional F-35 Joint Strike Fighters would enable the Air Force, which is now the smallest it has been in history, to counter the growing number of complex threats from sophisticated state actors and transnational terrorist groups.

DEPARTMENT OF EDUCATION

The Department of Education promotes improving student achievement and access to opportunity in elementary, secondary, and postsecondary education. The Department would refocus its mission on supporting States and school districts in their efforts to provide high quality education to all our students. Also, it would focus on streamlining and simplifying funding for college, while continuing to help make college education more affordable. The 2018 Budget places power in the hands of parents and families to choose schools that are best for their children by investing an additional $1.4 billion in school choice programs. It continues support for the Nation's most vulnerable populations, such as students with disabilities. Overall, the Department would support these investments and carry out its core mission while lowering costs to the taxpayer by reducing or eliminating funding for programs that are not effective, that duplicate other efforts, or that do not serve national needs.

The President's 2018 Budget provides $59 billion in discretionary funding for the Department of Education, a $9 billion or 13 percent reduction below the 2017 annualized CR level.

The President's 2018 Budget:

- Increases investments in public and private school choice by $1.4 billion compared to the 2017 annualized CR level, ramping up to an annual total of $20 billion, and an estimated $100 billion including matching State and local funds. This additional investment in 2018 includes a $168 million increase for charter schools, $250 million for a new private school choice program, and a $1 billion increase for Title I, dedicated to encouraging districts to adopt a system of student-based budgeting and open enrollment that enables Federal, State, and local funding to follow the student to the public school of his or her choice.

- Maintains approximately $13 billion in funding for IDEA programs to support students with special education needs. This funding provides States, school districts, and other grantees with the resources needed to provide high quality special education and related services to students and young adults with disabilities.

- Eliminates the $2.4 billion Supporting Effective Instruction State Grants program, which is poorly targeted and spread thinly across thousands of districts with scant evidence of impact.

- Eliminates the 21st Century Community Learning Centers program, which supports before- and after-school programs as well as summer programs, resulting in savings of $1.2 billion from the 2017 annualized CR level. The programs lacks strong evidence of meeting its objectives, such as improving student achievement.

- Eliminates the Federal Supplemental Educational Opportunity Grant program, a less well-targeted way to deliver need-based aid than the Pell Grant program, to reduce complexity in financial student aid and save $732 million from the 2017 annualized CR level.

- Safeguards the Pell Grant program by level funding the discretionary appropriation while proposing a cancellation of $3.9 billion from unobligated carryover funding, leaving the Pell program on sound footing for the next decade.

- Protects support for Historically Black Colleges and Universities and Minority-Serving Institutions, which provide opportunities for communities that are often underserved, maintaining $492 million in funding for programs that serve high percentages of minority students.

- Reduces Federal Work-Study significantly and reforms the poorly-targeted allocation to ensure funds go to undergraduate students who would benefit most.

- Provides $808 million for the Federal TRIO Programs and $219 million for GEAR UP, resulting in savings of $193 million from the 2017 annualized CR level. Funding to TRIO programs is reduced in areas that have limited evidence on the overall effectiveness in improving student outcomes. The Budget funds GEAR UP continuation awards only, pending the completion of an upcoming rigorous evaluation of a portion of the program.

- Eliminates or reduces over 20 categorical programs that do not address national needs, duplicate other programs, or are more appropriately supported with State, local, or private funds, including Striving Readers, Teacher Quality Partnership, Impact Aid Support Payments for Federal Property, and International Education programs.

DEPARTMENT OF ENERGY

The Department of Energy (DOE) is charged with ensuring the Nation's security and prosperity by addressing its energy, environmental, and nuclear challenges through transformative science and technology solutions. The Budget for DOE demonstrates the Administration's commitment to reasserting the proper role of what has become a sprawling Federal Government and reducing deficit spending. It reflects an increased reliance on the private sector to fund later-stage research, development, and commercialization of energy technologies and focuses resources toward early-stage research and development. It emphasizes energy technologies best positioned to enable American energy independence and domestic job-growth in the near to mid-term. It also ensures continued progress on cleaning up sites contaminated from nuclear weapons production and energy research and includes a path forward to accelerate progress on the disposition of nuclear waste. At the same time, the Budget demonstrates the Administration's strong support for the United States' nuclear security enterprise and ensures that we have a nuclear force that is second to none.

The President's 2018 Budget requests $28.0 billion for DOE, a $1.7 billion or 5.6 percent decrease from the 2017 annualized CR level. The Budget would strengthen the Nation's nuclear capability by providing a $1.4 billion increase above the 2017 annualized CR level for the National Nuclear Security Administration, an 11 percent increase.

The President's 2018 Budget:

- Provides $120 million to restart licensing activities for the Yucca Mountain nuclear waste repository and initiate a robust interim storage program. These investments would accelerate progress on fulfilling the Federal Government's obligations to address nuclear waste, enhance national security, and reduce future taxpayer burden.
- Supports the goals of moving toward a responsive nuclear infrastructure and advancing the existing program of record for warhead life extension programs through elimination of defense sequestration for the National Nuclear Security Administration (NNSA).
- Enables NNSA to begin to address its critical infrastructure maintenance backlog.
- Protects human health and the environment by providing $6.5 billion to advance the Environmental Management program mission of cleaning up the legacy of waste and contamination from energy research and nuclear weapons production, including addressing excess facilities to support modernization of the nuclear security enterprise.
- Eliminates the Advanced Research Projects Agency-Energy, the Title 17 Innovative Technology Loan Guarantee Program, and the Advanced Technology Vehicle Manufacturing Program because

the private sector is better positioned to finance disruptive energy research and development and to commercialize innovative technologies.

- Ensures the Office of Science continues to invest in the highest priority basic science and energy research and development as well as operation and maintenance of existing scientific facilities for the community. This includes a savings of approximately $900 million compared to the 2017 annualized CR level.

- Focuses funding for the Office of Energy Efficiency and Renewable Energy, the Office of Nuclear Energy, the Office of Electricity Delivery and Energy Reliability, and the Fossil Energy Research and Development program on limited, early-stage applied energy research and development activities where the Federal role is stronger. In addition, the Budget eliminates the Weatherization Assistance Program and the State Energy Program to reduce Federal intervention in State-level energy policy and implementation. Collectively, these changes achieve a savings of approximately $2 billion from the 2017 annualized CR level.

- Supports the Office of Electricity Delivery and Energy Reliability's capacity to carry out cybersecurity and grid resiliency activities that would help harden and evolve critical grid infrastructure that the American people and the economy rely upon.

- Continues the necessary research, development, and construction to support the Navy's current nuclear fleet and enhance the capabilities of the future fleet.

DEPARTMENT OF HEALTH AND HUMAN SERVICES

The Department of Health and Human Services (HHS) works to enhance the health and well-being of Americans by providing effective health and human services and by fostering sound, sustained advances in the sciences underlying medicine, public health, and social services. The Budget supports the core mission of HHS through the most efficient and effective health and human service programs. In 2018, HHS funds the highest priorities, such as: health services through community health centers, Ryan White HIV/AIDS providers, and the Indian Health Service; early care and education; and medical products review and innovation. In addition, it funds urgent public health issues, such as prescription drug overdose, and program integrity for Medicare and Medicaid. The Budget eliminates programs that are duplicative or have limited impact on public health and well-being. The Budget allows HHS to continue to support priority activities that reflect a new and sustainable approach to long-term fiscal stability across the Federal Government.

The President's 2018 Budget requests $69.0 billion for HHS, a $15.1 billion or 17.9 percent decrease from the 2017 annualized CR level. This funding level excludes certain mandatory spending changes but includes additional funds for program integrity and implementing the 21st Century CURES Act.

The President's 2018 Budget:

- Supports direct health care services, such as those delivered by community health centers, Ryan White HIV/AIDS providers, and the Indian Health Service. These safety net providers deliver critical health care services to low-income and vulnerable populations.

- Strengthens the integrity and sustainability of Medicare and Medicaid by investing in activities to prevent fraud, waste, and abuse and promote high quality and efficient health care. Additional funding for the Health Care Fraud and Abuse Control (HCFAC) program has allowed the Centers for Medicare & Medicaid Services in recent years to shift away from a "pay-and-chase" model toward identifying and preventing fraudulent or improper payments from being paid in the first place. The return on investment for the HCFAC account was $5 returned for every $1 expended from 2014-2016. The Budget proposes HCFAC discretionary funding of $751 million in 2018, which is $70 million higher than the 2017 annualized CR level.

- Supports efficient operations for Medicare, Medicaid, and the Children's Health Insurance Program and focuses spending on the highest priority activities necessary to effectively operate these programs.

- Supports substance abuse treatment services for the millions of Americans struggling with substance abuse disorders. The opioid epidemic, which took more than 33,000 lives in calendar year 2015, has a devastating effect on America's families and communities. In addition to funding Substance Abuse and Mental Health Services Administration substance abuse treatment activities, the Budget also includes a $500 million increase above 2016 enacted levels to expand opioid misuse prevention efforts and to increase access to treatment and recovery services to help Americans who are misusing opioids get the help they need.

- Recalibrates Food and Drug Administration (FDA) medical product user fees to over $2 billion in 2018, approximately $1 billion over the 2017 annualized CR level, and replaces the need for new budget authority to cover pre-market review costs. To complement the increase in medical product user fees, the Budget includes a package of administrative actions designed to achieve regulatory efficiency and speed the development of safe and effective medical products. In a constrained budget environment, industries that benefit from FDA's approval can and should pay for their share.

- Reduces the National Institutes of Health's (NIH) spending relative to the 2017 annualized CR level by $5.8 billion to $25.9 billion. The Budget includes a major reorganization of NIH's Institutes and Centers to help focus resources on the highest priority research and training activities, including: eliminating the Fogarty International Center; consolidating the Agency for Healthcare Research and Quality within NIH; and other consolidations and structural changes across NIH organizations and activities. The Budget also reduces administrative costs and rebalance Federal contributions to research funding.

- Reforms key public health, emergency preparedness, and prevention programs. For example, the Budget restructures similar HHS preparedness grants to reduce overlap and administrative costs and directs resources to States with the greatest need. The Budget also creates a new Federal Emergency Response Fund to rapidly respond to public health outbreaks, such as Zika Virus Disease. The Budget also reforms the Centers for Disease Control and Prevention through a new $500 million block grant to increase State flexibility and focus on the leading public health challenges specific to each State.

- Invests in mental health activities that are awarded to high-performing entities and focus on high priority areas, such as suicide prevention, serious mental illness, and children's mental health.

- Eliminates $403 million in health professions and nursing training programs, which lack evidence that they significantly improve the Nation's health workforce. The Budget continues to fund health workforce activities that provide scholarships and loan repayments in exchange for service in areas of the United States where there is a shortage of health professionals.

- Eliminates the discretionary programs within the Office of Community Services, including the Low Income Home Energy Assistance Program (LIHEAP) and the Community Services Block Grant (CSBG), a savings of $4.2 billion from the 2017 annualized CR level. Compared to other income support programs that serve similar populations, LIHEAP is a lower-impact program and is unable to demonstrate strong performance outcomes. CSBG funds services that are duplicative of other Federal programs, such as emergency food assistance and employment services, and is also a limited-impact program.

DEPARTMENT OF HOMELAND SECURITY

The Department of Homeland Security (DHS) has a vital mission: to secure the Nation from the many threats it faces. This requires the dedication of more than 240,000 employees in jobs that ensure the security of the U.S. borders, support the integrity of its immigration system, protect air travelers and national leaders, reduce the threat of cyber attacks, and stand prepared for emergency response and disaster recovery. The Budget prioritizes DHS law enforcement operations, proposes critical investments in frontline border security, and funds continued development of strong cybersecurity defenses. The Budget would aggressively implement the President's commitment to construct a physical wall along the southern border as directed by his January 25, 2017 Executive Order, and ensures robust funding for other important DHS missions.

The President's 2018 Budget requests $44.1 billion in net discretionary budget authority for DHS, a $2.8 billion or 6.8 percent increase from the 2017 annualized CR level. The Budget would allocate $4.5 billion in additional funding for programs to strengthen the security of the Nation's borders and enhance the integrity of its immigration system. This increased investment in the Nation's border security and immigration enforcement efforts now would ultimately save Federal resources in the future.

The President's 2018 Budget:

- Secures the borders of the United States by investing $2.6 billion in high-priority tactical infrastructure and border security technology, including funding to plan, design, and construct a physical wall along the southern border as directed by the President's January 25, 2017 Executive Order. This investment would strengthen border security, helping stem the flow of people and drugs illegally crossing the U.S. borders.

- Advances the President's plan to strengthen border security and immigration enforcement with $314 million to recruit, hire, and train 500 new Border Patrol Agents and 1,000 new Immigration and Customs Enforcement law enforcement personnel in 2018, plus associated support staff. These new personnel would improve the integrity of the immigration system by adding capacity to interdict those aliens attempting to cross the border illegally, as well as to identify and remove those already in the United States who entered illegally.

- Enhances enforcement of immigration laws by proposing an additional $1.5 billion above the 2017 annualized CR level for expanded detention, transportation, and removal of illegal immigrants.

These funds would ensure that DHS has sufficient detention capacity to hold prioritized aliens, including violent criminals and other dangerous individuals, as they are processed for removal.

- Invests $15 million to begin implementation of mandatory nationwide use of the E-Verify Program, an internet-based system that allows businesses to determine the eligibility of their new employees to work in the United States. This investment would strengthen the employment verification process and reduce unauthorized employment across the U.S.

- Safeguards cyberspace with $1.5 billion for DHS activities that protect Federal networks and critical infrastructure from an attack. Through a suite of advanced cyber security tools and more assertive defense of Government networks, DHS would share more cybersecurity incident information with other Federal agencies and the private sector, leading to faster responses to cybersecurity attacks directed at Federal networks and critical infrastructure.

- Restructures selected user fees for the Transportation Security Administration (TSA) and the National Flood Insurance Program (NFIP) to ensure that the cost of Government services is not subsidized by taxpayers who do not directly benefit from those programs. The Budget proposes to raise the Passenger Security Fee to recover 75 percent of the cost of TSA aviation security operations. The Budget proposes eliminating the discretionary appropriation for the NFIP's Flood Hazard Mapping Program, a savings of $190 million, to instead explore other more effective and fair means of funding flood mapping efforts.

- Eliminates or reduces State and local grant funding by $667 million for programs administered by the Federal Emergency Management Agency (FEMA) that are either unauthorized by the Congress, such as FEMA's Pre-Disaster Mitigation Grant Program, or that must provide more measurable results and ensure the Federal Government is not supplanting other stakeholders' responsibilities, such as the Homeland Security Grant Program. For that reason, the Budget also proposes establishing a 25 percent non-Federal cost match for FEMA preparedness grant awards that currently require no cost match. This is the same cost-sharing approach as FEMA's disaster recovery grants. The activities and acquisitions funded through these grant programs are primarily State and local functions.

- Eliminates and reduces unauthorized and underperforming programs administered by TSA in order to strengthen screening at airport security checkpoints, a savings of $80 million from the 2017 annualized CR level. These savings include reductions to the Visible Intermodal Prevention and Response program, which achieves few Federal law enforcement priorities, and elimination of TSA grants to State and local jurisdictions, a program intended to incentivize local law enforcement patrols that should already be a high priority for State and local partners. In addition, the Budget reflects TSA's decision in the summer of 2016 to eliminate the Behavior Detection Officer program, reassigning all of those personnel to front line airport security operations. Such efforts refocus TSA on its core mission of protecting travelers and ensuring Federal security standards are enforced throughout the transportation system.

DEPARTMENT OF HOUSING AND URBAN DEVELOPMENT

The Department of Housing and Urban Development (HUD) promotes decent, safe, and affordable housing for Americans and provides access to homeownership opportunities. This Budget reflects the President's commitment to fiscal responsibility while supporting critical functions that provide rental assistance to low-income and vulnerable households and help work-eligible families achieve self-sufficiency. The Budget also recognizes a greater role for State and local governments and the private sector to address community and economic development needs.

The President's 2018 Budget requests $40.7 billion in gross discretionary funding for HUD, a $6.2 billion or 13.2 percent decrease from the 2017 annualized CR level.

The President's 2018 Budget:

- Provides over $35 billion for HUD's rental assistance programs and proposes reforms that reduce costs while continuing to assist 4.5 million low-income households.

- Eliminates funding for the Community Development Block Grant program, a savings of $3 billion from the 2017 annualized CR level. The Federal Government has spent over $150 billion on this block grant since its inception in 1974, but the program is not well-targeted to the poorest populations and has not demonstrated results. The Budget devolves community and economic development activities to the State and local level, and redirects Federal resources to other activities.

- Promotes fiscal responsibility by eliminating funding for a number of lower priority programs, including the HOME Investment Partnerships Program, Choice Neighborhoods, and the Self-help Homeownership Opportunity Program, a savings of over $1.1 billion from the 2017 annualized CR level. State and local governments are better positioned to serve their communities based on local needs and priorities.

- Promotes healthy and lead-safe homes by providing $130 million, an increase of $20 million over the 2017 annualized CR level, for the mitigation of lead-based paint and other hazards in low-income homes, especially those in which children reside. This also funds enforcement, education, and research activities to further support this goal, all of which contributes to lower healthcare costs and increased productivity.

- Eliminates funding for Section 4 Capacity Building for Community Development and Affordable Housing, a savings of $35 million from the 2017 annualized CR level. This program is duplicative of efforts funded by philanthropy and other more flexible private sector investments.

- Supports homeownership through provision of Federal Housing Administration mortgage insurance programs.

DEPARTMENT OF THE INTERIOR

The Department of the Interior (DOI) is responsible for protecting and managing vast areas of U.S. lands and waters, providing scientific and other information about its natural resources, and meeting the Nation's trust responsibilities and other commitments to American Indians, Alaska Natives, and U.S.-affiliated island communities. The Budget requests an increase in funding for core energy development programs while supporting DOI's priority agency mission and trust responsibilities, including public safety, land conservation and revenue management. It eliminates funding for unnecessary or duplicative programs while reducing funds for lower priority activities, such as acquiring new lands.

The President's 2018 Budget requests $11.6 billion for DOI, a $1.5 billion or 12 percent decrease from the 2017 annualized CR level.

The President's 2018 Budget:

- Strengthens the Nation's energy security by increasing funding for DOI programs that support environmentally responsible development of energy on public lands and offshore waters. Combined with administrative reforms already in progress, this would allow DOI to streamline permitting processes and provide industry with access to the energy resources America needs, while ensuring taxpayers receive a fair return from the development of these public resources.

- Sustains funding for DOI's Office of Natural Resources Revenue, which manages the collection and disbursement of roughly $10 billion annually from mineral development, an important source of revenue to the Federal Treasury, States, and Indian mineral owners.

- Eliminates unnecessary, lower priority, or duplicative programs, including discretionary Abandoned Mine Land grants that overlap with existing mandatory grants, National Heritage Areas that are more appropriately funded locally, and National Wildlife Refuge fund payments to local governments that are duplicative of other payment programs.

- Supports stewardship capacity for land management operations of the National Park Service, Fish and Wildlife Service and Bureau of Land Management. The Budget streamlines operations while providing the necessary resources for DOI to continue to protect and conserve America's public lands and beautiful natural resources, provide access to public lands for the next generation of outdoor enthusiasts, and ensure visitor safety.

- Supports tribal sovereignty and self-determination across Indian Country by focusing on core funding and services to support ongoing tribal government operations. The Budget reduces funding for more recent demonstration projects and initiatives that only serve a few Tribes.

- Reduces funding for lower priority activities, such as new major acquisitions of Federal land. The Budget reduces land acquisition funding by more than $120 million from the 2017 annualized CR level and would instead focus available discretionary funds on investing in, and maintaining, existing national parks, refuges and public lands.

- Ensures that the National Park Service assets are preserved for future generations by increasing investment in deferred maintenance projects. Reduces funds for other DOI construction and major maintenance programs, which can rely on existing resources for 2018.

- Provides more than $900 million for DOI's U.S. Geological Survey to focus investments in essential science programs. This includes funding for the Landsat 9 ground system, as well as research and data collection that informs sustainable energy development, responsible resource management, and natural hazard risk reduction.

- Leverages taxpayer investment with public and private resources through wildlife conservation, historic preservation, and recreation grants. These voluntary programs encourage partnerships by providing matching funds that produce greater benefits to taxpayers for the Federal dollars invested.

- Budgets responsibly for wildland fire suppression expenses. The Budget would directly provide the full 10-year rolling average of suppression expenditures.

- Invests over $1 billion in safe, reliable, and efficient management of water resources throughout the western United States.

- Supports counties through discretionary funding for the Payments in Lieu of Taxes (PILT) program at a reduced level, but in line with average funding for PILT over the past decade.

DEPARTMENT OF JUSTICE

> The Department of Justice is charged with enforcing the laws and defending the interests of the United States, ensuring public safety against foreign and domestic threats, providing Federal leadership in preventing and controlling crime, seeking just punishment for those guilty of unlawful behavior, and ensuring the fair and impartial administration of justice for all Americans. The budget for the Department of Justice saves taxpayer dollars by consolidating, reducing, streamlining, and making its programs and operations more efficient. The Budget also makes critical investments to confront terrorism, reduce violent crime, tackle the Nation's opioid epidemic, and combat illegal immigration.
>
> The President's 2018 Budget requests $27.7 billion for the Department of Justice, a $1.1 billion or 3.8 percent decrease from the 2017 annualized CR level. This program level excludes mandatory spending changes involving the Crime Victims Fund and the Assets Forfeiture Fund. However, significant targeted increases would enhance the ability to address key issues, including public safety, law enforcement, and national security. Further, the Administration is concerned about so-called sanctuary jurisdictions and will be taking steps to mitigate the risk their actions pose to public safety.

The President's 2018 Budget:

- Strengthens counterterrorism, counterintelligence, and Federal law enforcement activities by providing an increase of $249 million, or 3 percent, above the 2017 annualized CR level for the Federal Bureau of Investigation (FBI). The FBI would devote resources toward its world-class cadre of special agents and intelligence analysts, as well as invest $61 million more to fight terrorism and combat foreign intelligence and cyber threats and address public safety and national security risks that result from malicious actors' use of encrypted products and services. In addition, the FBI would dedicate $35 million to gather and share intelligence data with partners and together with the Department of Defense (DOD) lead Federal efforts in biometric identity resolution, research, and development. The FBI would also spend an additional $9 million to provide accurate and timely response for firearms purchase background checks, and develop and refine evidence and data to target violent crime in some cities and communities.

- Supports efforts at the Department's law enforcement components by providing a combined increase of $175 million above the 2017 annualized CR level to target the worst of the worst criminal organizations and drug traffickers in order to address violent crime, gun-related deaths, and the opioid epidemic.

- Enhances national security and counterterrorism efforts by linking skilled prosecutors and intelligence attorneys with law enforcement investigations and the intelligence community to stay ahead of threats.

- Combats illegal entry and unlawful presence in the United States by providing an increase of nearly $80 million, or 19 percent, above the 2017 annualized CR level to hire 75 additional immigration judge teams to bolster and more efficiently adjudicate removal proceedings—bringing the total number of funded immigration judge teams to 449.

- Enhances border security and immigration enforcement by providing 60 additional border enforcement prosecutors and 40 deputy U.S. Marshals for the apprehension, transportation, and prosecution of criminal aliens.

- Supports the addition of 20 attorneys to pursue Federal efforts to obtain the land and holdings necessary to secure the Southwest border and another 20 attorneys and support staff for immigration litigation assistance.

- Assures the safety of the public and law enforcement officers by providing $171 million above the 2017 annualized CR level for additional short-term detention space to hold Federal detainees, including criminal aliens, parole violators, and other offenders awaiting trial or sentencing.

- Safeguards Federal grants to State, local, and tribal law enforcement and victims of crime to ensure greater safety for law enforcement personnel and the people they serve. Critical programs aimed at protecting the life and safety of State and local law enforcement personnel, including Preventing Violence Against Law Enforcement Officer Resilience and Survivability and the Bulletproof Vest Partnership, are protected.

- Eliminates approximately $700 million in unnecessary spending on outdated programs that either have met their goal or have exceeded their usefulness, including $210 million for the poorly targeted State Criminal Alien Assistance Program, in which two-thirds of the funding primarily reimburses four States for the cost of incarcerating certain illegal criminal aliens.

- Achieves savings of almost a billion dollars from the 2017 annualized CR level in Federal prison construction spending due to excess capacity resulting from an approximate 14 percent decrease in the prison population since 2013. However, the Budget provides $80 million above the 2017 annualized CR level for the activation of an existing facility to reduce high security Federal inmate overcrowding and a total of $113 million to repair and modernize outdated prisons.

- Increases bankruptcy-filing fees to produce an additional $150 million over the 2017 annualized CR level to ensure that those that use the bankruptcy court system pay for its oversight. By increasing quarterly filing fees, the total estimated United States Trustee Program offsetting receipts would reach $289 million in 2018.

DEPARTMENT OF LABOR

The Department of Labor fosters the welfare of wage earners, job seekers, and retirees by safeguarding their working conditions, benefits, and wages. With the need to rebuild the Nation's military without increasing the deficit, this Budget focuses the Department of Labor on its highest priority functions and disinvests in activities that are duplicative, unnecessary, unproven, or ineffective.

The President's 2018 Budget requests $9.6 billion for the Department of Labor, a $2.5 billion or 21 percent decrease from the 2017 annualized CR level.

The President's 2018 Budget:

- Expands Reemployment and Eligibility Assessments, an evidence-based activity that saves an average of $536 per claimant in unemployment insurance benefit costs by reducing improper payments and getting claimants back to work more quickly and at higher wages.

- Reduces funding for ineffective, duplicative, and peripheral job training grants. As part of this, eliminates the Senior Community Service Employment Program (SCSEP), for a savings of $434 million from the 2017 annualized CR level. SCSEP is ineffective in meeting its purpose of transitioning low-income unemployed seniors into unsubsidized jobs. As many as one-third of participants fail to complete the program and of those who do, only half successfully transition to unsubsidized employment.

- Focuses the Bureau of International Labor Affairs on ensuring that U.S. trade agreements are fair for American workers. The Budget eliminates the Bureau's largely noncompetitive and unproven grant funding, which would save at least $60 million from the 2017 annualized CR level.

- Improves Job Corps for the disadvantaged youth it serves by closing centers that do a poor job educating and preparing students for jobs.

- Decreases Federal support for job training and employment service formula grants, shifting more responsibility for funding these services to States, localities, and employers.

- Helps States expand apprenticeship, an evidence-based approach to preparing workers for jobs.

- Refocuses the Office of Disability Employment Policy, eliminating less critical technical assistance grants and launching an early intervention demonstration project to allow States to test and evaluate methods that help individuals with disabilities remain attached to or reconnect to the labor market.

- Eliminates the Occupational Safety and Health Administration's unproven training grants, yielding savings of almost $11 million from the 2017 annualized CR level and focusing the agency on its central work of keeping workers safe on the job.

DEPARTMENT OF STATE, USAID, AND TREASURY INTERNATIONAL PROGRAMS

The Department of State, the U.S. Agency for International Development (USAID), and the Department of the Treasury's International Programs help to advance the national security interests of the United States by building a more democratic, secure, and prosperous world. The Budget for the Department of State and USAID diplomatic and development activities is being refocused on priority strategic objectives and renewed attention is being placed on the appropriate U.S. share of international spending. In addition, the Budget seeks to reduce or end direct funding for international organizations whose missions do not substantially advance U.S. foreign policy interests, are duplicative, or are not well-managed. Additional steps will be taken to make the Department and USAID leaner, more efficient, and more effective. These steps to reduce foreign assistance free up funding for critical priorities here at home and put America first.

The President's 2018 Budget requests $25.6 billion in base funding for the Department of State and USAID, a $10.1 billion or 28 percent reduction from the 2017 annualized CR level. The Budget also requests $12.0 billion as Overseas Contingency Operations funding for extraordinary costs, primarily in war areas like Syria, Iraq, and Afghanistan, for an agency total of $37.6 billion. The 2018 Budget also requests $1.5 billion for Treasury International Programs, an $803 million or 35 percent reduction from the 2017 annualized CR level.

The President's 2018 Budget:

- Maintains robust funding levels for embassy security and other core diplomatic activities while implementing efficiencies. Consistent with the Benghazi Accountability Review Board recommendation, the Budget applies $2.2 billion toward new embassy construction and maintenance in 2018. Maintaining adequate embassy security levels requires the efficient and effective use of available resources to keep embassy employees safe.

- Provides $3.1 billion to meet the security assistance commitment to Israel, currently at an all-time high; ensuring that Israel has the ability to defend itself from threats and maintain its Qualitative Military Edge.

- Eliminates the Global Climate Change Initiative and fulfills the President's pledge to cease payments to the United Nations' (UN) climate change programs by eliminating U.S. funding related to the Green Climate Fund and its two precursor Climate Investment Funds.

- Provides sufficient resources on a path to fulfill the $1 billion U.S. pledge to Gavi, the Vaccine Alliance. This commitment helps support Gavi to vaccinate hundreds of millions of children in low-resource countries and save millions of lives.

- Provides sufficient resources to maintain current commitments and all current patient levels on HIV/AIDS treatment under the President's Emergency Plan for AIDS Relief (PEPFAR) and maintains funding for malaria programs. The Budget also meets U.S. commitments to the Global Fund for AIDS, Tuberculosis, and Malaria by providing 33 percent of projected contributions from all donors, consistent with the limit currently in law.

- Shifts some foreign military assistance from grants to loans in order to reduce costs for the U.S. taxpayer, while potentially allowing recipients to purchase more American-made weaponry with U.S. assistance, but on a repayable basis.

- Reduces funding to the UN and affiliated agencies, including UN peacekeeping and other international organizations, by setting the expectation that these organizations rein in costs and that the funding burden be shared more fairly among members. The amount the U.S. would contribute to the UN budget would be reduced and the U.S. would not contribute more than 25 percent for UN peacekeeping costs.

- Refocuses economic and development assistance to countries of greatest strategic importance to the U.S. and ensures the effectiveness of U.S. taxpayer investments by rightsizing funding across countries and sectors.

- Allows for significant funding of humanitarian assistance, including food aid, disaster, and refugee program funding. This would focus funding on the highest priority areas while asking the rest of the world to pay their fair share. The Budget eliminates the Emergency Refugee and Migration Assistance account, a duplicative and stovepiped account, and challenges international and non-governmental relief organizations to become more efficient and effective.

- Reduces funding for the Department of State's Educational and Cultural Exchange (ECE) Programs. ECE resources would focus on sustaining the flagship Fulbright Program, which forges lasting connections between Americans and emerging leaders around the globe.

- Improves efficiency by eliminating overlapping peacekeeping and security capacity building efforts and duplicative contingency programs, such as the Complex Crises Fund. The Budget also eliminates direct appropriations to small organizations that receive funding from other sources and can continue to operate without direct Federal funds, such as the East-West Center.

- Recognizes the need for State and USAID to pursue greater efficiencies through reorganization and consolidation in order to enable effective diplomacy and development.

- Reduces funding for multilateral development banks, including the World Bank, by approximately $650 million over three years compared to commitments made by the previous administration. Even with the proposed decreases, the U.S. would retain its current status as a top donor while saving taxpayer dollars.

DEPARTMENT OF TRANSPORTATION

The Department of Transportation (DOT) is responsible for ensuring a fast, safe, efficient, accessible, and convenient transportation system that meets our vital national interests and enhances the quality of life of the American people today, and into the future. The Budget request reflects a streamlined DOT that is focused on performing vital Federal safety oversight functions and investing in nationally and regionally significant transportation infrastructure projects. The Budget reduces or eliminates programs that are either inefficient, duplicative of other Federal efforts, or that involve activities that are better delivered by States, localities, or the private sector.

The President's 2018 Budget requests $16.2 billion for DOT's discretionary budget, a $2.4 billion or 13 percent decrease from the 2017 annualized CR level.

The President's 2018 Budget:

- Initiates a multi-year reauthorization proposal to shift the air traffic control function of the Federal Aviation Administration to an independent, non-governmental organization, making the system more efficient and innovative while maintaining safety. This would benefit the flying public and taxpayers overall.

- Restructures and reduces Federal subsidies to Amtrak to focus resources on the parts of the passenger rail system that provide meaningful transportation options within regions. The Budget terminates Federal support for Amtrak's long distance train services, which have long been inefficient and incur the vast majority of Amtrak's operating losses. This would allow Amtrak to focus on better managing its State-supported and Northeast Corridor train services.

- Limits funding for the Federal Transit Administration's Capital Investment Program (New Starts) to projects with existing full funding grant agreements only. Future investments in new transit projects would be funded by the localities that use and benefit from these localized projects.

- Eliminates funding for the Essential Air Service (EAS) program, which was originally conceived of as a temporary program nearly 40 years ago to provide subsidized commercial air service to rural airports. EAS flights are not full and have high subsidy costs per passenger. Several EAS-eligible communities are relatively close to major airports, and communities that have EAS could be served by other existing modes of transportation. This proposal would result in a discretionary savings of $175 million from the 2017 annualized CR level.

- Eliminates funding for the unauthorized TIGER discretionary grant program, which awards grants to projects that are generally eligible for funding under existing surface transportation formula programs, saving $499 million from the 2017 annualized CR level. Further, DOT's Nationally Significant Freight and Highway Projects grant program, authorized by the FAST Act of 2015, supports larger highway and multimodal freight projects with demonstrable national or regional benefits. This grant program is authorized at an annual average of $900 million through 2020.

DEPARTMENT OF THE TREASURY

The Department of the Treasury is charged with maintaining a strong economy, promoting conditions that enable economic growth and stability, protecting the integrity of the financial system, and managing the U.S. Government's finances and resources effectively. The Budget will bring renewed discipline to the Department by focusing resources on collecting revenue, managing the Nation's debt, protecting the financial system from threats, and combating financial crime and terrorism financing.

The President's 2018 Budget requests $12.1 billion in discretionary resources for the Department of the Treasury's domestic programs, a $519 million or 4.1 percent decrease from the 2017 annualized CR level. This program level excludes mandatory spending changes involving the Treasury Forfeiture Fund.

The President's 2018 Budget:

- Preserves key operations of the Internal Revenue Service (IRS) to ensure that the IRS could continue to combat identity theft, prevent fraud, and reduce the deficit through the effective enforcement and administration of tax laws. Diverting resources from antiquated operations that are still reliant on paper-based review in the era of electronic tax filing would achieve significant savings, a funding reduction of $239 million from the 2017 annualized CR level.

- Strengthens cybersecurity by investing in a Department-wide plan to strategically enhance existing security systems and preempt fragmentation of information technology management across the bureaus, positioning Treasury to anticipate and nimbly respond in the event of a cyberattack.

- Prioritizes funding for Treasury's array of economic enforcement tools. Key Treasury programs that freeze the accounts of terrorists and proliferators, implement sanctions on rogue nations, and link law enforcement agencies with financial institutions are critical to the continued safety and financial stability of the Nation.

- Eliminates funding for Community Development Financial Institutions (CDFI) Fund grants, a savings of $210 million from the 2017 annualized CR level. The CDFI Fund was created more than 20 years ago to jump-start a now mature industry where private institutions have ready access to the capital needed to extend credit and provide financial services to underserved communities.

- Empowers the Treasury Secretary, as Chairperson of the Financial Stability Oversight Council, to end taxpayer bailouts and foster economic growth by advancing financial regulatory reforms that promote market discipline and ensure the accountability of financial regulators.

- Shrinks the Federal workforce and increases its efficiency by redirecting resources away from duplicative policy offices to staff that manage the Nation's finances.

DEPARTMENT OF VETERANS AFFAIRS

> The Department of Veterans Affairs (VA) provides health care and a wide variety of benefits to military veterans and their survivors. The 2018 Budget fulfills the President's commitment to the Nation's veterans by requesting the resources necessary to provide the support our veterans have earned through sacrifice and service to our Nation. The Budget significantly increases funding for VA Medical Care so that VA can continue to meet the ever-growing demand for health care services while building an integrated system of care that strengthens services within VA and makes effective use of community services. The Budget request includes increased funding for and extension of the Veterans Choice Program, making it easier for eligible veterans to access the medical care they need, close to home.
>
> The President's 2018 Budget requests $78.9 billion in discretionary funding for VA, a $4.4 billion or 6 percent increase from the 2017 enacted level. The Budget also requests legislative authority and $3.5 billion in mandatory budget authority in 2018 to continue the Veterans Choice Program.

The President's 2018 Budget:

- Ensures the Nation's veterans receive high-quality health care and timely access to benefits and services. An estimated 11 million veterans participate in VA programs. This Budget provides the resources necessary to ensure veterans receive the care and support earned through their service to the Nation.

- Provides a $4.6 billion increase in discretionary funding for VA health care to improve patient access and timeliness of medical care services for over nine million enrolled veterans. This funding would enable the Department to provide a broad range of primary care, specialized care, and related medical and social support services to enrolled veterans, including services that are uniquely related to veterans' health and special needs.

- Extends and funds the Veterans Choice Program to ensure that every eligible veteran continues to have the choice to seek care at VA or through a private provider. Without action, this critical program will expire in August 2017, which would result in veterans having fewer choices of where to receive care.

- Supports VA programs that provide services to homeless and at-risk veterans and their families to help keep them safe and sheltered.

- Provides access to education benefits, enhanced services, and other programs to assist veterans' transition to civilian life. VA partners with other agencies to provide critical training, support services, and counseling throughout a veteran's transition and their post-military career.

- Continues critical investments aimed at optimizing productivity and transforming VA's claims processes. Provides resources to reduce the time required to process and adjudicate veterans' disability compensation claims.
- Invests in information technology to improve the efficiency and efficacy of VA services. Provides sufficient funding for sustainment, development, and modernization initiatives that would improve the quality of services provided to veterans and avoid the costs of maintaining outdated, inefficient systems.

ENVIRONMENTAL PROTECTION AGENCY

> The Environmental Protection Agency (EPA) is responsible for protecting human health and the environment. The budget for EPA reflects the success of environmental protection efforts, a focus on core legal requirements, the important role of the States in implementing the Nation's environmental laws, and the President's priority to ease the burden of unnecessary Federal regulations that impose significant costs for workers and consumers without justifiable environmental benefits. This would result in approximately 3,200 fewer positions at the agency. EPA would primarily support States and Tribes in their important role protecting air, land, and water in the 21st Century.
>
> The President's 2018 Budget requests $5.7 billion for the Environmental Protection Agency, a savings of $2.6 billion, or 31 percent, from the 2017 annualized CR level.

The President's 2018 Budget:

- Provides robust funding for critical drinking and wastewater infrastructure. These funding levels further the President's ongoing commitment to infrastructure repair and replacement and would allow States, municipalities, and private entities to continue to finance high priority infrastructure investments that protect human health. The Budget includes $2.3 billion for the State Revolving Funds, a $4 million increase over the 2017 annualized CR level. The Budget also provides $20 million for the Water Infrastructure Finance and Innovation Act program, equal to the funding provided in the 2017 annualized CR. This credit subsidy could potentially support $1 billion in direct Federal loans.

- Discontinues funding for the Clean Power Plan, international climate change programs, climate change research and partnership programs, and related efforts—saving over $100 million for the American taxpayer compared to 2017 annualized CR levels. Consistent with the President's America First Energy Plan, the Budget reorients EPA's air program to protect the air we breathe without unduly burdening the American economy.

- Reins in Superfund administrative costs and emphasizes efficiency efforts by funding the Hazardous Substance Superfund Account at $762 million, $330 million below the 2017 annualized CR level. The agency would prioritize the use of existing settlement funds to clean up hazardous waste sites and look for ways to remove some of the barriers that have delayed the program's ability to return sites to the community.

- Avoids duplication by concentrating EPA's enforcement of environmental protection violations on programs that are not delegated to States, while providing oversight to maintain consistency and assistance across State, local, and tribal programs. This reduces EPA's Office of Enforcement and Compliance Assurance budget to $419 million, which is $129 million below the 2017 annualized CR level.

- Better targets EPA's Office of Research and Development (ORD) at a level of approximately $250 million, which would result in a savings of $233 million from the 2017 annualized CR level. ORD would prioritize activities that support decision-making related to core environmental statutory requirements, as opposed to extramural activities, such as providing STAR grants.

- Supports Categorical Grants with $597 million, a $482 million reduction below 2017 annualized CR levels. These lower levels are in line with the broader strategy of streamlining environmental protection. This funding level eliminates or substantially reduces Federal investment in State environmental activities that go beyond EPA's statutory requirements.

- Eliminates funding for specific regional efforts such as the Great Lakes Restoration Initiative, the Chesapeake Bay, and other geographic programs. These geographic program eliminations are $427 million lower than the 2017 annualized CR levels. The Budget returns the responsibility for funding local environmental efforts and programs to State and local entities, allowing EPA to focus on its highest national priorities.

- Eliminates more than 50 EPA programs, saving an additional $347 million compared to the 2017 annualized CR level. Lower priority and poorly performing programs and grants are not funded, nor are duplicative functions that can be absorbed into other programs or that are State and local responsibilities. Examples of eliminations in addition to those previously mentioned include: Energy Star; Targeted Airshed Grants; the Endocrine Disruptor Screening Program; and infrastructure assistance to Alaska Native Villages and the Mexico Border.

NATIONAL AERONAUTICS AND SPACE ADMINISTRATION

The National Aeronautics and Space Administration (NASA) is responsible for increasing understanding of the universe and our place in it, advancing America's world-leading aerospace technology, inspiring the Nation, and opening the space frontier. The Budget increases cooperation with industry through the use of public-private partnerships, focuses the Nation's efforts on deep space exploration rather than Earth-centric research, and develops technologies that would help achieve U.S. space goals and benefit the economy.

The President's 2018 Budget requests $19.1 billion for NASA, a 0.8 percent decrease from the 2017 annualized CR level, with targeted increases consistent with the President's priorities.

The President's 2018 Budget:

- Supports and expands public-private partnerships as the foundation of future U.S. civilian space efforts. The Budget creates new opportunities for collaboration with industry on space station operations, supports public-private partnerships for deep-space habitation and exploration systems, funds data buys from companies operating small satellite constellations, and supports work with industry to develop and commercialize new space technologies.

- Paves the way for eventual over-land commercial supersonic flights and safer, more efficient air travel with a strong program of aeronautics research. The Budget provides $624 million for aeronautics research and development.

- Reinvigorates robotic exploration of the Solar System by providing $1.9 billion for the Planetary Science program, including funding for a mission to repeatedly fly by Jupiter's icy ocean moon Europa and a Mars rover that would launch in 2020. To preserve the balance of NASA's science portfolio and maintain flexibility to conduct missions that were determined to be more important by the science community, the Budget provides no funding for a multi-billion-dollar mission to land on Europa. The Budget also supports initiatives that use smaller, less expensive satellites to advance science in a cost-effective manner.

- Provides $3.7 billion for continued development of the Orion crew vehicle, Space Launch System, and associated ground system, to send American astronauts on deep-space missions. To accommodate increasing development costs, the Budget cancels the multi-billion-dollar Asteroid Redirect Mission. NASA will investigate approaches for reducing the costs of exploration missions to enable a more expansive exploration program.

- Provides $1.8 billion for a focused, balanced Earth science portfolio that supports the priorities of the science and applications communities, a savings of $102 million from the 2017 annualized CR level. The Budget terminates four Earth science missions (PACE, OCO-3, DSCOVR

Earth-viewing instruments, and CLARREO Pathfinder) and reduces funding for Earth science research grants.

- Eliminates the $115 million Office of Education, resulting in a more focused education effort through NASA's Science Mission Directorate. The Office of Education has experienced significant challenges in implementing a NASA-wide education strategy and is performing functions that are duplicative of other parts of the agency.
- Restructures a duplicative robotic satellite refueling demonstration mission to reduce its cost and better position it to support a nascent commercial satellite servicing industry, resulting in a savings of $88 million from the 2017 annualized CR level.
- Strengthens NASA's cybersecurity capabilities, safeguarding critical systems and data.

SMALL BUSINESS ADMINISTRATION

The Small Business Administration (SBA) ensures that small businesses have the tools and resources needed to start and develop their operations, drive U.S. competitiveness, and help grow the economy. The President is committed to assisting small businesses succeed through reducing the regulatory and tax burdens that can impede the development of small firms. The Budget increases efficiency through responsible reductions to redundant programs and by eliminating programs that deliver services better provided by the private sector.

The President's 2018 Budget requests $826.5 million for SBA, a $43.2 million or 5.0 percent decrease from the 2017 annualized CR level.

The President's 2018 Budget:

- Supports more than $45 billion in loan guarantees to assist America's small business owners with access to affordable capital to start or expand their businesses.

- Strengthens SBA's outreach center programs by reducing duplicative services, coordinating best practices, and investing in communities that would benefit from SBA's business center support. As a result, SBA would be better positioned to strengthen local partnerships and more efficiently serve program participants while achieving savings over the 2017 annualized CR level.

- Supports over $1 billion in disaster relief lending to businesses, homeowners, renters, and property owners to help American communities recover quickly in the wake of declared disasters. Through the disaster loan program, SBA is able to provide affordable, accessible, and immediate direct assistance to those hardest hit when disaster strikes.

- Achieves $12 million in cost savings from the 2017 annualized CR level through identifying and eliminating those SBA grant programs where the private sector provides effective mechanisms to foster local business development and investment. Eliminations include PRIME technical assistance grants, Regional Innovation Clusters, and Growth Accelerators.

- Provides training and support services for transitioning service members and veterans to promote entrepreneurship and business ownership. These programs help to fulfill the President's commitment to support the Nation's veterans by providing business counseling, lending, and contracting assistance.

- Maintains $28 million in microloan financing and technical assistance to help serve, strengthen, and sustain the smallest of small businesses and startups.

- Allows SBA to advocate and assist small businesses in accessing Federal contracts and small business research opportunities Government-wide.

Summary Tables

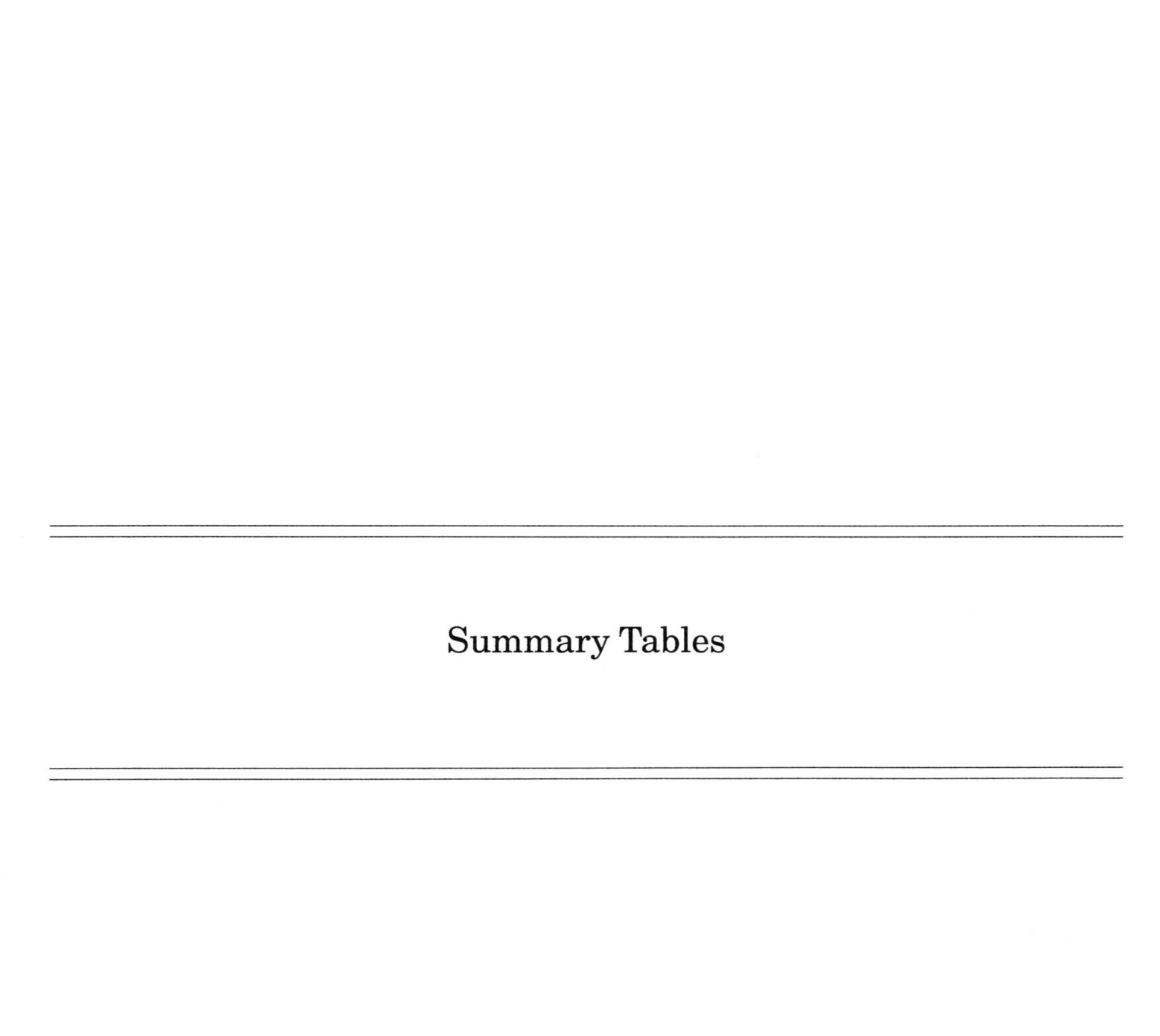

Table 1. Proposed Discretionary Caps for 2018 Budget

(Budget authority in billions of dollars)

	Caps 2017	Caps 2018
Current Law Base Caps: [1]		
Defense	551	549
Non-Defense	519	516
Total, Current Law Base Caps	**1,070**	**1,065**
Proposed Base Cap Changes: [2]		
Defense	*+25*	*+54*
Non-Defense	*–15*	*–54*
Total, Proposed Changes	***+10***	....
Proposed Base Caps:		
Defense	576	603
Non-Defense	504	462
Total, Proposed Base Caps	**1,080**	**1,065**
Enacted and Proposed Cap Adjustments:		
Overseas Contingency Operations (OCO) [2]	89	77
Emergency Funding	3	....
Program Integrity	2	2
Disaster Relief	8	7
Total, Cap Adjustments	**102**	**86**
Total, Discretionary Budget Authority	**1,181**	**1,151**
21st Century CURES appropriations [3]	*1*	*1*

[1] The caps presented here are equal to the levels specified for 2017 and 2018 in the Balanced Budget and Emergency Deficit Control Act of 1985, as amended (BBED-CA). The 2017 caps were revised in the Bipartisan Budget Act of 2015 and the 2018 caps include OMB estimates of Joint Committee enforcement (also known as "sequestration").

[2] The Administration proposes an increase in the existing defense caps for 2017 and 2018 that is offset with decreases to the non-defense caps. About 60 percent of the 2017 defense increase is offset by non-defense decreases in 2017 while the entire defense increase in 2018 is offset by non-defense decreases. An additional $5 billion in defense funding is proposed as OCO in 2017.

[3] The 21st Century CURES Act permitted funds to be appropriated each year for certain activities outside of the discretionary caps so long as the appropriations were specifically provided for the authorized purposes. These amounts are displayed outside of the discretionary totals for this reason.

Table 2. 2018 Discretionary Overview by Major Agency

(Net discretionary BA in billions of dollars)

	2017 CR/Enacted [1,2]	2018 Request [2]	2018 Request Less 2017 CR/Enacted Dollar	2018 Request Less 2017 CR/Enacted Percent
Base Discretionary Funding:				
Cabinet Departments:				
Agriculture [3]	22.6	17.9	–4.7	–20.7%
Commerce	9.2	7.8	–1.5	–15.7%
Defense	521.7	574.0	+52.3	+10.0%
Education	68.2	59.0	–9.2	–13.5%
Energy	29.7	28.0	–1.7	–5.6%
National Nuclear Security Administration	*12.5*	*13.9*	*+1.4*	*+11.3%*
Other Energy	*17.2*	*14.1*	*–3.1*	*–17.9%*
Health and Human Services [4]	77.7	65.1	–12.6	–16.2%
Homeland Security	41.3	44.1	+2.8	+6.8%
Housing and Urban Development (HUD):				
HUD gross total (excluding receipts)	*46.9*	*40.7*	*–6.2*	*–13.2%*
HUD receipts [5]	*–10.9*	*–9.0*	*+1.9*	*N/A*
Interior	13.2	11.6	–1.5	–11.7%
Justice (DOJ):				
DOJ program level (excluding offsets)	*28.8*	*27.7*	*–1.1*	*–3.8%*
DOJ mandatory spending changes (CHIMPs)	*–8.5*	*–11.5*	*–2.9*	*N/A*
Labor	12.2	9.6	–2.5	–20.7%
State, U.S. Agency for International Development (USAID), and Treasury International Programs [3]	38.0	27.1	–10.9	–28.7%
Transportation	18.6	16.2	–2.4	–12.7%
Treasury	11.7	11.2	–0.5	–4.4%
Veterans Affairs	74.5	78.9	+4.4	+5.9%
Major Agencies:				
Corps of Engineers	6.0	5.0	–1.0	–16.3%
Environmental Protection Agency	8.2	5.7	–2.6	–31.4%
General Services Administration	0.3	0.5	+0.3	N/A
National Aeronautics and Space Administration	19.2	19.1	–0.2	–0.8%
Small Business Administration	0.9	0.8	–*	–5.0%
Social Security Administration [4]	9.3	9.3	+*	+0.2%
Other Agencies	29.4	26.5	–2.9	–9.8%
Subtotal, Discretionary Base Budget Authority	**1,068.1**	**1,065.4**	**–2.7**	**–0.3%**
Cap Adjustment Funding:				
Overseas Contingency Operations:				
Defense	65.0	64.6	–0.4	–0.6%
State and USAID	19.2	12.0	–7.2	–37.4%
Other Agencies	0.2	....	–0.2	–100.0%
Subtotal, Overseas Contingency Operations	84.3	76.6	–7.8	–9.2%
Emergency Requirements:				
Transportation	1.0	....	–1.0	–100.0%
Corps of Engineers	1.0	....	–1.0	–100.0%
Other Agencies	0.7	....	–0.7	–100.0%
Subtotal, Emergency Requirements	2.7	....	–2.7	–100.0%
Program Integrity:				
Health and Human Services	0.4	0.4	+0.1	+17.3%
Social Security Administration	1.2	1.5	+0.3	+26.8%
Subtotal, Program Integrity	1.5	1.9	+0.4	+24.5%

Table 2. 2018 Discretionary Overview by Major Agency—Continued

(Net discretionary BA in billions of dollars)

	2017 CR/Enacted [1,2]	2018 Request [2]	2018 Request Less 2017 CR/Enacted Dollar	2018 Request Less 2017 CR/Enacted Percent
Disaster Relief: [6]				
Homeland Security and Other Agencies	6.7	7.4	+0.7	+9.7%
Housing and Urban Development	1.4	....	–1.4	–100.0%
Subtotal, Disaster Relief	8.1	7.4	–0.8	–9.4%
Subtotal, Cap Adjustment Funding	**96.7**	**85.9**	**–10.8**	**–11.2%**
Total, Discretionary Budget Authority	**1,164.8**	**1,151.2**	**–13.6**	**–1.2%**
Memorandum: 21st Century CURES appropriations [7]				
Health and Human Services	0.9	1.1	+0.2	+21.1%

* $50 million or less.

[1] The 2017 CR/Enacted column reflects enacted appropriations and levels of continuing appropriations provided under the Continuing Appropriations Act, 2017 (Division C of Public Law 114–223, as amended by Division A of Public Law 114–254) that are due to expire on April 28. The levels presented here are the amounts OMB scores under the caps; therefore, the levels for 2017 may differ in total from those on Table 1.

[2] Enacted, continuing, and proposed changes in mandatory programs (CHIMPs) are included in both 2017 and 2018. Some agency presentations in this volume where noted reflect a program level that excludes these amounts.

[3] Funding for Food for Peace Title II Grants is included in the State, USAID, and Treasury International programs total. Although the funds are appropriated to the Department of Agriculture, the funds are administered by USAID.

[4] Funding from the Hospital Insurance and Supplementary Medical Insurance trust funds for administrative expenses incurred by the Social Security Administration that support the Medicare program are included in the Health and Human Services total and not in the Social Security Administration total.

[5] HUD receipt levels for 2018 are a placeholder and subject to change as detailed estimates under the Administration's economic and technical assumptions for the full Budget are finalized.

[6] The Balanced Budget and Emergency Deficit Control Act of 1985 authorizes an adjustment to the discretionary spending caps for appropriations that are designated by the Congress as being for "disaster relief" provided those appropriations are for activities carried out pursuant to a determination under the Robert T. Stafford Disaster Relief and Emergency Assistance Act. Currently, based on enacted and continuing appropriations, OMB estimates the total adjustment available for disaster funding for 2018 at $7,366 million. Further details, including any revisions necessary to account for final 2017 appropriations and the specific amounts of disaster relief funding requested for individual agencies in 2018 authorized to administer disaster relief programs, will be provided in subsequent Administration proposals.

[7] The 21st Century CURES Act permitted funds to be appropriated each year for certain activities outside of the discretionary caps so long as the appropriations were specifically provided for the authorized purposes. These amounts are displayed outside of the discretionary totals for this reason.

Table 3. Major 2018 Budget Changes from Current Law

(Budget authority in billions of dollars)

	2018 Caps [1]		Change:	
	Current Law [2]	Proposed	Dollars	Percent
Discretionary Categories:				
Defense	549	603	+54	+10%
Non-Defense	516	462	–54	–10%
Total, 2018 Base Caps	**1,065**	**1,065**	....	....

* $500 million or less.

[1] Only base funding caps are represented on this table and cap adjustments permitted by the Balanced Budget and Emergency Deficit Control Act of 1985 for overseas contingency operations, disaster relief, program integrity, and emergency requirements are excluded.

[2] The current law caps are equal to the levels specified for 2018 in the Balanced Budget and Emergency Deficit Control Act of 1985, including OMB estimates for Joint Committee enforcement (also known as "sequestration").

Table 4. Major 2017 Changes from Security Supplemental Request

(Budget authority in billions of dollars)

	2017 Caps Current Law	2017 Caps Proposed [1]	Change: Dollars	Change: Percent
Discretionary Categories:				
Defense	551	576	+25	+5%
Non-Defense	519	504	–15	–3%
Major Changes:				
Border Wall and implementation of Executive Orders	....	*3*	*+3*	*N/A*
Other Non-Defense programs	*519*	*501*	*–18*	*–3%*
Total, 2018 Base Caps	1,070	1,080	+10	+1%
Cap Adjustments:				
Defense Overseas Contingency Operations (OCO)	65	70	+5	+8%

[1] The Administration proposes an increase in the existing defense cap for 2017 that is partially offset with a decrease to the non-defense cap while an additional $5 billion defense request in 2017 is requested as OCO.